edible gifts

edible gifts

Jane Lyster

NH
NEW
HOLLAND

Contents

Introduction   7

Materials   10

The food gifter's workshop 12
Kitchen equipment   12
Craft equipment   16

Presentation techniques   18
Wrapping in paper   18
Making boxes   19
Box templates   21
Decorating a box   27

Sweet gifts •   31
Chocolate eggs   33
Amaretti biscuits   37
Shortbread   40
Box of cake decorations   45
Toffee apples and pears   52
Sugared ring doughnuts   56
Creams   61
Lemon marmalade   65
Fudge   69
Strawberry jam   70
Macaroons   74
Florentines   77

Not so sweet • 79

Homemade pasta	83
Pesto	87
Sun-dried tomato pesto	88
Breadsticks	91
Tasty oils	94
Water biscuits	99
Blue cheese and port pâté	101
Living salad bowl	102
Pickles	106
Marinated olives	109
Tasty salts	113
Two sauces in a pack	117
Plum and apple chutney	121

Drinks • 123

Elderflower cordial	125
Tea infusions	127
Cocktails	131
Champagne and flower cocktail	132
Cocktails in measures	134
Limoncello	139
Sloe gin and sloe gin chocolate	140

Christmas gifts • 143

Edible gift tags	144
Mulled wine bags	149
Turkish delight	150
Sugar mice	155
Chocolate truffles	156
Roasted nuts	160
Christmas tree biscuits	164
Gingerbread men	169
Gingerbread house	173

Introduction

This book contains projects for you to create and give to your friends while helping you to develop your own artistic style. Lots of the recipes here are old favourites that have been reinvented to be enjoyed anew.

The beauty of making edible gifts is that you can create beautiful, unique gifts, often at a fraction of the price of anything you would find in the shops. But often the nicest gifts are those that come as a complete surprise, especially if they have been made by hand. These gifts really can be anything: jars of blackberry jam with a loaf of freshly baked bread or a tray of ready-to-plant-out tomato plants. The reason for giving is just to say 'I'm thinking of you' and however wobbly, unset or rock-hard crunchy, it's a pleasure to receive anything that a friend has taken the trouble to make with you in mind.

Of course in the world we live in today there is no need to make a thing, as every conceivable item can be purchased. 'Homemade' doesn't always suggest luxury or desirability. What if your carefully crafted gift turns out to be a catastrophe? Fear not. These projects are very simple and I hope that by my own experimentation I have ironed out the disaster potential.

Presents are given and received the whole year round although Christmas is the time when most people think of making delicious edible treats for their friends and family. However, anyone who loves baking and creating in the kitchen will soon find any excuse to make some of the projects in this book, whether it's a birthday, a wedding, a moving house gift or simply a little something to cheer up a friend.

There is always a rush of excitement and delight that comes when you produce a beautiful gift for a loved one. I love the thought of going out into the countryside to pick a basket of blackberries or sloes, coming home with them as if I am carrying unearthed treasures. Back in my kitchen I set myself up at the table. A pot of tea and the afternoon radio play are my companions. Slowly I prepare

my found jewels, picking over each one to look for defects and bruising and sorting into three piles: the perfect specimen pile, the middling pile and the not-so-sure-if-it-lasted-the-journey-home pile. As I work I consider what these piles will become. Shall I make jam, or drown then in alcohol? Who can I give them to or share them with? Will I manage to get them as far as someone else before I have to just sample a little more to make sure it tastes just right?

Making personalized gifts for your friends really will give you as much pleasure as receiving a present yourself and once you have mastered a few very simple techniques, you'll soon be hooked on handmade treats. Use the projects in this book as inspiration and you'll begin to look at all sorts of produce and packaging in a whole new light.

Materials

I like to use the best quality materials and ingredients, as I believe they can help to make the cooking and wrapping easier. It also makes the gifts seem a bit more special. That's not to say that secondhand bits and bobs that you find and collect on the way are unworthy. It's more about using exactly the right grade of flour to make pasta making a bit easier, or choosing a quality pencil that will keep its point for longer. A full range of materials at your fingertips really does cut down wasted hours at the shops, so being prepared is always useful. I always keep my kitchen cupboards stocked with a range of flours, sugars, good-quality chocolate and olive oils and I've always got fresh butter, eggs, lemons and fresh herbs to hand – so whipping up a batch of biscuity treats is never a problem.

Materials for decorating and wrapping are probably ones that you already have lying around the home but it's always good to be on the alert for useful finds. It's that magpie thing. The collector in you should be able to recognize the potential in the discarded item. Think of buttons and beads which can be stitched or glued over the surface of the lid of a box to make it extra special; odd lengths of ribbon to be wound around bottles, jars and hold together bundles of just-baked breadsticks; paper that was wrapped around a gift given to you, that you have carefully unwrapped, folded and stored for another day just as your grandmother would have done. Then there are fragments of lace and cloth from a past era, which give a homely, vintage feel. These are the treasures that you can't buy. A trove of trinkets takes a while to gather, but these odds and ends are worth their weight in gold. Being individual and different from the norm is what makes your gift unique.

Materials for wrapping and decorating

Rolls of coloured cellophane and cellophane bags

Wrapping paper

Coloured tissue paper

Coloured ribbons and fabric scraps

Balls of wool

Stencils

Paints, coloured pens and pencils

Varnish

Beads, buttons, sequins etc

The food gifter's workshop

The food gifter's workshop is essentially the kitchen, although if you don't have a table in your kitchen, at some point you will have to move to an area of the house where there is one.

One of the most important things is to clear your space ready for working. Most professional kitchens churn out food like a well oiled machine, and I am sure this is down to having a well organized space. Clearing space, having everything ready and prepping your ingredients beforehand will make all the difference to how smoothly the projects run. You don't want to boil your sugar to the right temperature and pour it into your moulds only to discover that you can't find your string, otherwise before you know it, you'll have sugar mice without tails. So remember, clear the decks and all will run smoothly.

Kitchen tools are worth investing in and need to be looked after. There is no end of kitchen gadgetry available these days and, let's face it, if you love cooking you probably enjoy browsing around kitchen shops. Some of these items will make your life easier, others won't, so think carefully before splashing out on some high-tech piece of equipment. Here are my essential pieces of equipment.

Kitchen equipment

SUGAR THERMOMETER For making jams, toffee, fudge or any other heated sugary treats.

KNIVES You can't beat a good sharp knife when preparing food. For most of these recipes the most useful ones are a paring knife, a chef's knife, and a pallet knife.

CUTTER SHAPES A set of circular biscuit cutters is a mainstay for any cook intent on baking and biscuit making. My advice would be to collect any shapes that take your fancy.

ICING BAG AND PIPING NOZZLES Acquire a good quality icing bag as they are really worth investing in; the cheaper ones tend to allow melted butter and cream to seep through the cloth.

ROLLING PIN The normal wooden rolling pins are great although you can also get marble ones. I have just discovered the silicone ones for rolling sugar fondants and think it's really worth having one, as the texture of the fondant after rolling is beautifully smooth.

COOLING TRAY Cooling trays are very important for drying out fondant cream, crystallized flowers and cooling hot biscuits, shortbreads etc.

STORAGE JARS Make sure you have a good selection of different-sized storage jars that can be tightly sealed.

MOULDS Pretty moulds are a joy to collect. Get a good selection together as they are fun to use and add endless possibilities to making fondants and chocolates.

HAND BLENDER Hand blenders have a very sharp little blade that whizzes around and so purées food in half the time that it would take by hand.

FOOD PROCESSOR Food processors are useful for making a whole range of goodies. They cut down the amount of time you need to spend on the project, and you can make in bulk. Ideal for cakes, mixing pâtés and pesto.

PESTLE AND MORTAR This is a beautiful gadget if you have the time because it really is worth pounding your own herbs and spices. The heavier the base the better as it then stays still while you pound away at your mixture.

Craft equipment

Once you have made your delicious gifts, you will want to present them in your own unique packaging. Below are some of the tools that will help you to make beautiful boxes, labels and decorations.

SCISSORS You need one pair of scissors for cutting cloth and one pair for cutting paper. If you try to use the paper ones for cloth you will find the experience hard work. It is also worth investing in a range of interesting scissors. You can get really funky sets with loads of different cutting edges for paper from good craft shops.

CRAFT KNIFE AND SELF-HEALING CUTTING MAT Make sure your craft knife is as sharp and straight as possible to give you a great, crisply edged result. Cutting mats are usually marked out with a grid for accurate cutting.

BRUSHES You can buy cheap brushes but I do recommend that you invest in some good quality ones. Painting is made much easier if you have a range of heads that are either sable or synthetic sable.

PENCILS Do not fall into the idea that any old pencil will do. A pencil with a good lead will help with the finished result. In my opinion the best pencils to use are either a 2B or3B soft lead, as when sharp you get a good, fine line but if left to a round edge you can draw a nice, soft line.

RUBBER STAMPS AND INK PADS Rubber stamps can be bought at most high street craft suppliers or you can make your own. Ink pads come in a variety of colours.

SEWING KIT You don't need a huge sewing kit but a few pins and needles, a tape measure and a pair of good sharp cloth scissors will all come in handy.

Presentation techniques

The right wrapping always makes a gift more beautiful, but wrapping presents is not always as easy as you might think. It's something about cutting the correct amount and shape of paper to start with, placing the gift in the right position and then being able to hold the paper tightly around the item while ripping off the tape in small strips and then getting them to stick in the right place. It's all about practice; wrapping gifts is after all down to technique. With time you will be able to master what might at first have seemed the hardest of techniques. Everything becomes easier and you will find that making gifts for friends becomes a pleasure and not so much of a chore.

Wrapping in paper

There are so many types of paper you can use to wrap gifts. Don't be fooled by the very cheapest as these are often rather thin so rip and tear, making the process a misery. Make sure that you choose slightly thicker paper, but do think about all the other papers that are available to us. There are old telephone directories for small gifts once the new one has been delivered through your door. Consider using maps, yesterday's newspaper, magazines, instruction manuals or large sheets of brown paper that you have printed on. How about wrapping your offering in large leaves tied with string or making a bag for your gift to live in that is an extra present in itself? Try layering one paper with a bold print under a finer tracing or parchment paper.

MARBLING

Marbling is fun to do and so easy, you don't need to worry about the outcome – but it can get messy so be prepared. It works by getting paint to float on the surface of water, which you then gently stir and manipulate to form a pattern. Then you lay your paper on the swirling paint and it adheres to your paper. Untreated newsprint or sugar paper work best as they are porous and so provide a good surface. Add 100 ml (3½ fl oz) of methyl cellulose to 4 litres (7 pints) of cold water in an old washing up bowl. Mix well and leave it to stand for an hour. Use acrylic paint and water down to the consistency of pancake batter. Now either drizzle or splatter the paint onto the surface of the water mixture in the bowl. When you have covered the surface of the water, lay your paper so that it floats on the solution. Let go of it and make sure that there are no air bubbles under the surface. Gently lift it from the solution and hang it out to dry on a washing line.

Making boxes

Be on the look out for all types of boxes because they are so useful. You could use them as they are or deconstruct them to use as templates for your own boxes in your chosen paper or card. You could also consider using other vessels for delivering your gifts such as picture frames, old trays, cups and saucers, teapots, old bottles, vases and odd glasses.

CONSTRUCTING A PACKAGE

When constructing a box or package in card or paper one of the things to remember is the importance of a sharp, crisp fold. This will make any construction you make work much better. One way to achieve this is to fold the length of the edge down over a book or table or up over a ruler. Once you have established where the fold is you can now reinforce this by folding at this point and lightly pressing the edge of the ruler over the crease starting from the bottom nearest you up to the top edge while holding the bottom of the fold with your thumb to the table; it's a little like ironing – in fact you could use a cool iron gently to do the same job if that suits you better. The finish it will give to the end result is really worthwhile.

How to make a box

A box is a wonderful structure, not only is it a pleasure or challenge to make it can also be a great vessel to transport goodies from one place to another. You have not only lovingly made the contents of the box, but have also spent time considering how it will be presented and then spent time building the receptacle. A very happy marriage of edible and craft based gift.

Here are a few patterns or rather box nets, which you can either trace or photocopy to produce a box of the right size for your food. It might be a good idea to do a thin photocopy of the nets you like as they are and then make up to see the size of the box. The nets can be either copied larger or smaller. Only then will you know if it works for your gift. Don't be frightened these are easy, if in doubt just copy one onto a scrap piece of paper and have a go at gluing together, before you cut up your beautiful sheet of paper.

Points to remember

- Use a very sharp scalpel, steel rule and a cutting board or good scissors to cut out. Accuracy is everything here.
- It's very important to fold all the creases before gluing.
- Use the right glue for the job – good quality paper/card glue is best.
- Get some paper clips ready to hold the joins in place or hold in place until ready.

Now all you need to do is work out which shaped box you need to hold your precious goods.

Box templates

Illustrations are not drawn to scale.

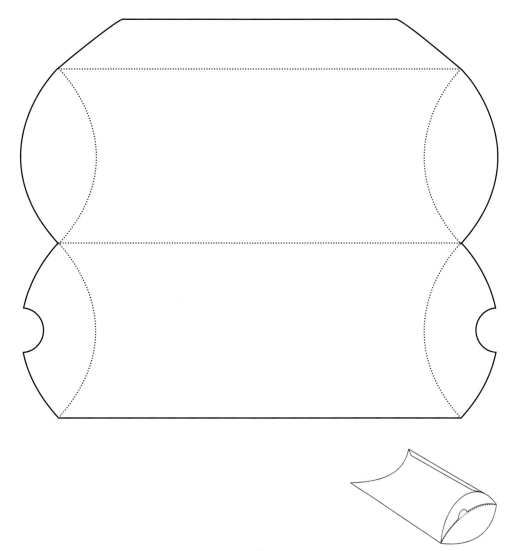

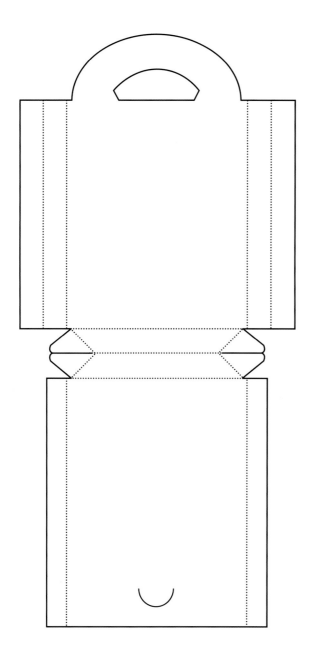

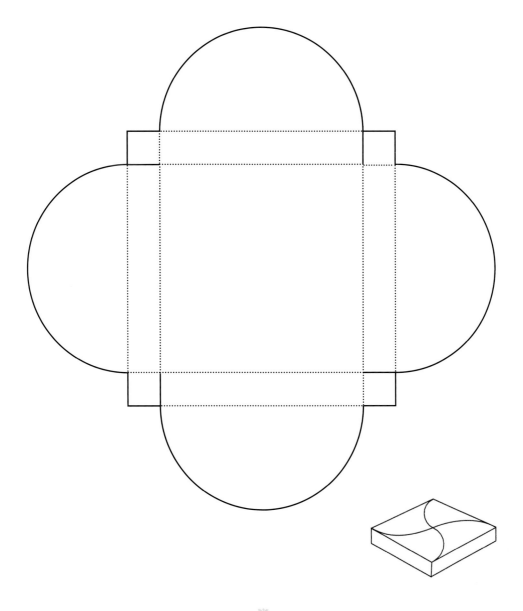

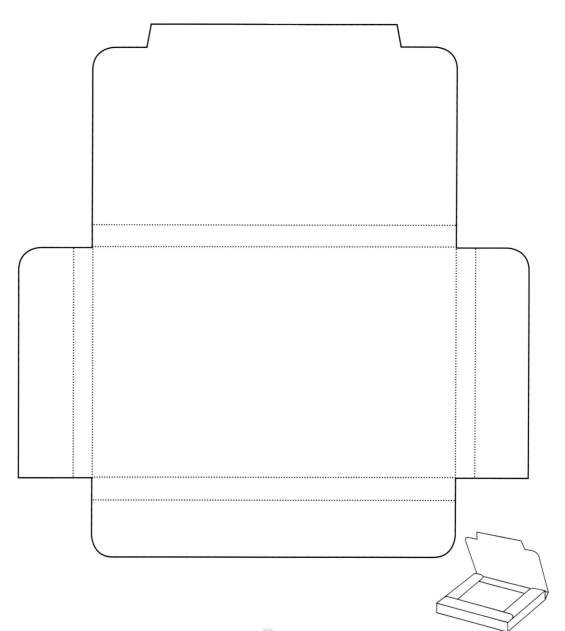

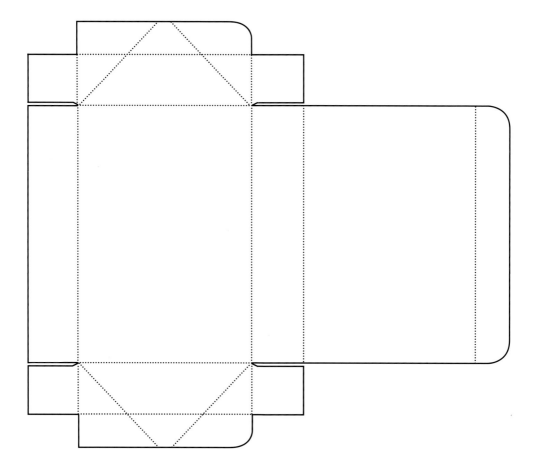

Cutting

Fit a new blade onto a good-quality craft knife each time you start a new project. A steel ruler and a cutting mat will also make all the difference to the finished cut. Place the paper you wish to cut on the mat and position the ruler. Hold the ruler in place with your thumb and forefinger and lightly drag the blade down the length of the cut from top to bottom. Repeat this with a pressure, again running the knife towards you. If you are working with thick board it might take a few cuts. This is invaluable when tracing around a box you have deconstructed and wish to re-make using another type of card.

Decorating a box

Curling / scrolling

Curling, or scrolling, has a long history; it is the art of rolling thin strips of paper into a sort of paper filigree that emulates ironwork. In the eighteenth century it became popular for ladies of leisure as it was considered not too complex for their gentle natures! It is formed by rolling tiny, narrow strips of paper around a cocktail stick or something similar and then leaving them to uncurl slightly before gluing them on their side edges to a base paper or other items such a box lid. You can slowly build up the curls to form a pattern or picture. This works best if you place lots of them together and build up a solid surface texture. White paper on a white background can look very beautiful and sophisticated.

Bows and paper pom-poms

These really make a difference to the final touches of a gift. I find it easiest to tie a knot first and then continue with the bow as that way you are not trying to keep the ribbon tight at the same time. If you make a series of bows you can place them on top of one another for a glorious effect. For a paper pom-pom use seven sheets of tissue paper on top of each other and fold them into pleats, first one way and then the other. Cut the ends in tassel points or round them off. Now either staple through the centre or secure with wire. Gently tease out the layers of tissue from each other to produce a ball.

SEWING

This book only contains a small amount of sewing. It can either be done by hand or machine. The only stitch used is a running stitch so there's nothing too complicated. If you are very good at sewing you can really go to town by embroidering some of your gift tags.

COLOURS

When choosing a colour scheme for your gift tags and wrapping be careful not to overdo it. The best rule to remember is that less is more. Over-complicate your palette and the colours will take over from the structural and visual look of the gift. To help you decide on your scheme choose two or three colours that fit in with the product you have made. That's not to say that a huge range of colours don't go well together, just take it easy.

Sweet gifts

When I think of edible gifts I nearly always think of sweet things – shortbread, jams and marmalades, chocolates and biscuits are sure to bring a smile to anyone's lips. This chapter has plenty of ideas for that special sweet-toothed someone.

Chocolate eggs

Decorated eggs are a traditional Easter gift and some of the examples are so beautiful it is hard to even consider painting your own. Use a range of quail, chicken, duck and goose eggs blown from their shells, fill with chocolate, then hand paint the eggs and arrange in pretty egg cups.

You will need

A range of bird eggs

Good-quality chocolate

Sharp pin

Piping bag with small nozzle

Egg cups

1 First wipe the outside of the eggs so that they are ready for blowing. Have some bowls to hand for the empty eggs (so they don't roll off the table and break) and for the blown egg. Using the sharp pin, you need to pierce a small hole in the top and bottom of your egg, measuring about 3 mm (1/8 in). Blowing from the top hole, blow the contents of the egg out of the bottom hole into the bowl below. Continue in this way until you have blown all the eggs you need to give as gifts.

2 Wash the eggs thoroughly inside and out in plenty of warm water. Rinse well and leave to drain and dry, then, using edible glue, place a tiny circle of tissue paper over one of the holes and place open hole side up in an egg cup.

3 Now melt the chocolate in a glass bowl over a saucepan of simmering water. Once it has just melted – be careful that it does not overheat and burn – remove from the heat and leave to rest for a few minutes to cool.

4 Place the chocolate into an icing bag with a small nozzle and carefully pipe the chocolate into the egg. You will need to very gently tap the bottom of the egg on the table and roll the egg around to make sure the chocolate really fills the empty shell. Once full, place in an egg cup until the chocolate has set. Now glue over the remaining hole in the same way as before.

Decorating and giftwrapping

You will need

Paintbrushes

Acrylic paints

Spray varnish

Egg cups

Cellophane and ribbon (optional)

You can keep the decoration simple on these eggs or really go to town. An egg painted with simple stripes or spots looks great. You can either go freeform and just start painting an overall colour, which can be over-painted when dry, or with a soft pencil you can mark out your pattern and then fill in the different areas. Once dry, spray with varnish so that the paint is coated with a protective layer. Arrange in egg cups and then wrap in cellophane tied with ribbon, if desired.

Amaretti biscuits

My husband claims that he doesn't like biscuits or cakes, yet if I make a batch of these I need to keep them hidden.

You will need

2 tsp amaretto

1 egg white

185 g (6½ oz) ground almonds

250 g (9 oz) caster sugar

Icing sugar (confectioners' sugar), for dusting

1 Preheat the oven to 180°C/350°F/gas 4. Grease some sheets of baking parchment and place on baking trays. In a bowl lightly whisk together the amaretto and egg white.

2 In another bowl, mix together the ground almonds and caster sugar and make a well in the centre. Pour the whisked egg whites into the well. Gently knead the mixture by hand in the bowl, then move to a surface lightly dusted with sieved icing sugar. Divide the mixture into 40 small balls and place on the parchment-lined baking trays.

3 Cook in the oven for about 10 minutes. Remove when golden brown and while still very hot, sprinkle with icing sugar and leave to cool on the baking trays. Store in an airtight jar.

Wrapping

Wait until the amaretti biscuits are completely cool before you wrap them. You can buy either plain or printed tissue paper – if you can only get hold of plain paper, try personalizing it by printing with rubber stamps.

Cut the paper into small squares, about 15 x 15 cm (6 x 6 in). Wrap each biscuit in a square of tissue paper and twist at the top. Place them into a clear cellophane bag and tie around the top with a piece of ribbon. You can then make your own label to add to the bag.

Shortbread

There are two trains of thought on this one: either strawberries should be served just with cream or with a little crunch provided, in which case a few shortbread biscuits are a must. My sister argues that strawberries should really only be served with a generous sprinkling of caster sugar; I on the other hand rather like the addition of crunch instead of the sugar. Either way strawberries are really only best freshly picked in the summer.

You will need

160 g (5½ oz) plain flour (all-purpose flour)
40 g (1½ oz) soft brown sugar
125 g (4 oz) butter
40 g (1½ oz) semolina flour
Caster sugar, for sprinkling

1 Preheat the oven to 160°C/325°F/gas mark 3 and lightly grease a couple of baking sheets.

2 In a bowl cream together the sugar and butter, then blend in the rest of the ingredients and turn out onto a lightly floured surface. Gently knead to form soft smooth dough. As it's so short this dough will be rather hard to work with.

3 Carefully roll out to a thickness of about 1 cm (½ in) then, using a biscuit cutter shape of your choice of about 3 cm (1½ in) in diameter, cut out as many biscuits as possible. Reroll and cut more biscuits until all the dough is used up.

4 Arrange the biscuits onto the greased baking sheets and place in the centre of your hot oven for about 15 minutes or until just staring to turn a golden brown. On removal from the oven immediately sprinkle with caster sugar so that it sticks to the biscuits. Cool on the baking sheets for 20 minutes and then remove with a pallet knife to a wire tray. This recipe makes about 24 biscuits depending on the biscuit cutter size.

Wrapping

I like to present these a basket just large enough to hold a punnet of strawberries, a small glass pot of double cream and the freshly baked shortbread biscuits in a clear cellophane bag.

Box of cake decorations

This is a great present for someone who loves to bake. They will last for several weeks and are ready when needed for a celebration.

Fondant

You will need

200 g (7 oz) white marshmallows

1 tbsp water

400 g (14 oz) icing sugar (confectioners' sugar)

1 Melt the marshmallows and water in a glass bowl over simmering water. Take off the heat and stir the mixture. Leave to cool for five minutes or so. Transfer to a large mixing bowl and sieve in about half of the icing sugar to help stiffen the paste. When the fondant is firm enough to handle, transfer to a tabletop liberally sprinkled with icing sugar. Knead the fondant while slowly sieving more icing sugar over the mixture as necessary. When the fondant is stiff divide into six balls and dye each small ball with food colouring. You might find that you need to add a little more icing sugar to each small piece at this point. Place the fondant lumps in plastic bags and store in the fridge until needed.

2 When you are ready to create your shapes, simply roll out with a rolling pin and cut out shapes with cutters.

Crystallized edible flowers

You will need

Edible flowers such as begonia, hibiscus, marigold,
mint flower, nasturtium, pineapple sage, violet,
chrysanthemums, rose, rosehip or sweet pea
1 egg white
Caster sugar, for sprinkling

1 Place the caster sugar in a bowl and lightly whisk the egg white in another bowl. Using a clean, soft paintbrush paint a thin layer of the egg white all over each flower, then sprinkle with caster sugar. Leave on a wire rack to dry overnight.

Chocolate leaves

You will need

Chocolate of your choice
A selection of leaves

1 Make sure that the leaves you choose are not poisonous and that they are wiped clean before use. Once clean lay them out ready for painting.

2 Melt the chocolate in a bowl over a saucepan of hot water. Take the bowl containing the melted chocolate off the hot water. Use a small clean paintbrush to paint the melted chocolate over the underside of the leaves. Place into the fridge for about 15 minutes and once set, peel the leaf away from the chocolate.

Chocolate shapes

These are any shape you fancy, depending on your skill with the piping bag. The more you practise the better you will get and you can always scrap it all, re-melt the chocolate and start all over again.

You will need

A mixture of different chocolates

A piping bag and set of piping nozzles

1 Melt the chocolate in a double boiler or in a bowl over a pan of hot water. Take the bowl containing the melted chocolate off the hot water. Leave to rest away from the heated water for a few minutes.

2 Now you need to temper the chocolate. You will need a pastry scraper for this. Tempering means that you pour the chocolate onto a flat surface and move it around with the pastry scraper to help cool it down, with the result that when you put it into the piping bag it will not be too runny and run away.

3 Fill the piping bag with the tempered chocolate and start to draw some shapes on the parchment paper. You may need to practise a few to get them right. You can also sprinkle with hundreds and thousands. Allow to cool before gently peeling away from the paper.

Toffee apples and pears

Apples and pears coated in rich toffee – a naughty but nice treat.

You will need

6 toffee apple sticks

6 apples or pears

200 ml (7 fl oz) water

220 g (8 oz) soft brown sugar

40 g (1½ oz) butter

2 tsp vanilla balsamic vinegar

1 Wash your fruit and push the sticks into the bottom at the core. In a large heavy-based pan, heat the water and sugar until just boiling. Add the butter and vinegar and boil until the mixture reaches a temperature of 138°C (280°F). This could take up to 20 minutes.

2 Dip the fruit into the toffee, holding onto the sticks, then leave on a plate until the toffee has set. When coating the fruit, I like to let the toffee run down the sides so the fruit sits in a sticky puddle. When set, this makes an extra treat. Speed up setting by putting the coated fruit in the fridge.

Wrapping

There are really only two ways to give these away: either on a tray when they are to be consumed within moments of being made, or wrapped in cellophane or baking parchment and tied with a ribbon.

Sugared ring doughnuts

I love nothing more than a doughnut and homemade ones are way beyond compare. If you manage to keep these to give away I take my hat off to you.

You will need

200 g (7 oz) self-raising flour

40 g (1½ oz) caster sugar

40 g (1½ oz) margarine/butter

30 ml (1 fl oz) milk

1 egg

1 tsp vanilla essence

1 lemon, zest only

Pinch salt

Oil, for deep-frying

1 Get yourself prepared by having a plate of caster sugar ready for tossing the doughnuts in and a plate to let them rest for a moment before the sugar stage so that the hot oil residue does not melt the sugar on contact.

2 Cream together the sugar and margarine in a large bowl. Mix the milk and egg together in a jug and add to the creamed butter and sugar. Now slowly sieve in the flour, baking powder and salt until you have a dough-like mixture.

3 On a lightly floured table, roll the dough out to 1 cm (½ in) thickness, using a 6-cm (2½-in) round cutter. Cut out as many doughnuts as possible then, using a 4-cm (1½-in) cutter, cut out the doughnut holes. Keep rerolling the dough until you have used it all up.

4 Heat the oil to a temperature of 190°C/375°F in a large, deep saucepan. Carefully lower a few doughnuts at a time into the hot oil. Cook for about 2 minutes on each side or until golden brown. Using a slotted spoon, remove from the heat and place on a plate for a few minutes before tossing in caster sugar.

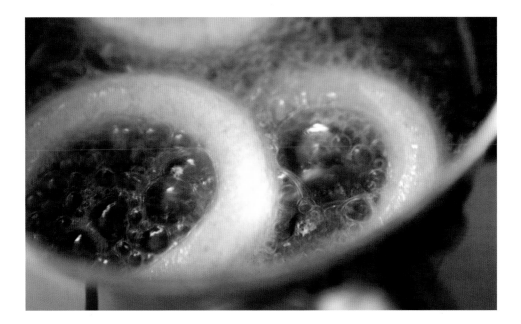

Wrapping

I'm not sure where I first heard about the doughnuts on a string game, but the gist of it is that you string up the doughnuts then try to eat them with your hands behind your back, it's huge fun! For this game it's best if you make ring doughnuts, which are then ready to be hung on a string. Use plain cotton string and tie each doughnut through its hole with a loose knot. Place them in a box along with the playing instructions.

Creams

If you or your friends loved Parma violets as children, then these little sweet treats will take you back to a bygone age. If they were too floral for your taste buds then try some peppermint, fresh lemon or wake-up coffee ones.

Once made, these creams looked so beautiful all laid out that I couldn't resist the idea of them being set onto a picture frame with some made-up butterfly names. I came up with Violet Blue, Lemon Tip, Coffee Admiral, Rose Geranium Lady and Peppermint White.

You will need

1 egg, white only

200 g (7 oz) icing sugar (confectioners' sugar)

Peppermint essence

Violet essence

Coffee essence

Rose geranium essence

Lemon essence

1 Beat the egg white in a large bowl until it just starts to stiffen. Slowly sieve the icing sugar into the egg and stir until the mixture forms a stiff paste. Divide the paste into five equal portions and add a few drops of each of the flavours to each of the portions. You might at this point need to add a little more icing sugar so sieve in a tiny amount at a time.

2 Gently knead each ball of paste for a couple of moments and then sandwich between two sheets of waxed or silicon paper. Roll out to 1 cm (½ in) thick and, using a bite-sized or 2 cm (¾ in) cutter, stamp out as many creams as you can. Leave to dry out overnight on a wire tray before wrapping.

Wrapping

You will need

1 picture frame

Piece of card

Edible glue

1 egg white, lightly whisked

Cellophane

Ribbon (optional)

Using edible glue, glue the butterflies in place onto a piece of stiff card that has been cut to the right size to fit the picture frame. Alternatively you can use a little whisked egg white. Wrap the picture frame in clear cellophane to protect the creams and add a ribbon, if desired.

Lemon marmalade

This will make about 4 kilos (9 lbs) of marmalade, so there will be plenty to share and even keep one or two jars for yourself. The delicate lace edges on the jars might look complicated but they are just a 10 row repeat pattern so once you can work out the 10 rows you will be rolling. If you can't knit just buy a length of lace. It's only a tiny running stitch to attach them neatly to the edge of a circle of cloth.

You will need

1.5 kg (3½ lb) unwaxed lemons

3 litres (5 pints) water

2.5 kg (5 ½ lb) sugar

1 Wash the lemons and pick out the stalk end. Either zest the peel from the lemons or, using a potato peeler, peel them, making sure not to peel any of the white pith. Slice the peel into fine strips.

2 Cut the peeled lemons in half and squeeze out all the juice. Save all the pips into a small bowl. Scoop out the remaining lemons, leaving the pith behind. Roughly chop the pith and place into a square of muslin with the pips and tie up into a bag.

3 Chop the remaining pulp and place into a large pan with the bag of pith and pips and strained lemon juice. Add the water. Bring it all to the boil over a low heat and simmer for about two hours. The peel should be soft and the liquid reduced by about half.

4 Remove the bag and add the sugar. Stir until the sugar has dissolved. Bring to a rapid boil, continue to boil until setting point has been reached – this should take 15–20 minutes. Test this by placing a small amount of marmalade onto a cold saucer. Leave for a couple of minutes, push with your finger, if a thick skin has formed it is done. Leave to cool for 30 minutes before placing in a sterilized jar.

Wrapping

You will need

A small amount of 4 ply cotton

2 mm (US 0) knitting needles

20 cm (8 in) white cotton fabric

Needle and sewing thread

Cast on 6 sts.

1st Row: K3, YO, K2 tog, YO, K1.

2nd Row: Knit.

3rd Row: K4, YO, K2 tog, YO, K1.

4th Row: Knit.

5th Row: K5, YO, K2 tog, YO, K1.

6th Row: Knit.

7th Row: K6 , YO, K2 tog, YO, K1.

8th Row: Cast off 4 sts, K4.

Repeat rows 1–8.

1 Using a crochet hook make a length of chain to tie the fabric lid in place

2 Draw around your jam jar lid on a piece of paper to make a pattern leaving a hem allowance of 2 cm (¾ in). Use this to cut out the cloth lid for your jar, do one for each jar of marmalade you have made. Turn a small hem using a small running stitch. Knit your edge to fit around the hem of your jam jar cover. Stitch the knitted lace edge around the hem with a loose over stitch. Place on your jar and tie with the length of chain you have crocheted.

Fudge

This is the substance that started me cooking and sharing. As I have now discovered, the sugar thermometer is an essential piece of equipment – I can make fudge that sets every time now.

You will need

175 g (6 oz) dark soft brown sugar

200 g (7 oz) light muscovado sugar,

450 g (1 lb) condensed milk

50 g (2 oz) unsalted butter

100 g (3½ oz) plain/milk chocolate

1 tsp natural vanilla extract

150 ml (5 fl oz) pint water

1 Place the dark soft brown sugar, light muscovado sugar and condensed milk into a large saucepan and heat gently, stirring until the sugar dissolves. Bring to the boil and continue to boil until the temperature reaches 230°C/450°F on a sugar thermometer.

    2 Remove from the heat add the chocolate and butter, leave to cool slightly and then sit the saucepan in a larger saucepan of iced water and beat until the mixture becomes thick and creamy. It can start to set rather quickly but just keep going and flatten the top with the back of a spoon. Pour into a greased 20 cm (8 in) square tin. Leave to set for at least 30 minutes. Mark into squares with a knife and leave until set. Cut into pieces and store in an airtight container.

Wrapping

This stuff reminds all of us of the sweet shop so place into little plastic bags and make some homemade labels stating the ingredients and weight, or little pictures of the contents. Then instead of using sticky tape or ribbon I made card labels that fold over the opening to hold the bags together, punching holes in the top and lacing though the holes with raffia.

Strawberry jam

Knitted strawberry hats are easy to make for jam (jelly) and evoke a smile to all that see them. Of course you could always knit orange hats for marmalade!

You will need

1 kg (2 lb 2 oz) strawberries
1 kg (2 lb 2 oz) preserving sugar

Hull the strawberries and wash. Layer with the sugar and set aside in a cool place for 24 hours. Place in a large pan and bring to the boil for 5 minutes. Leave for 48 hours in a cool place and then bring to the boil again, this time boiling until the mixture has reached setting point. Leave for 30 minutes to cool slightly and pour into sterilized jars.

Wrapping

You will need

3.5 mm (US 10) knitting needles
Small amount of double knitting weight yarn

Strawberry hat leaves

Cast on 50 stitches.
Row 1: Knit.
Row 2: Purl.
Repeat rows 1 and 2 until you have 8 rows of stocking stitch.
Row 11: Knit row (K3, K2 tog repeat to end)

Row 12: purl
Row 13: (K2, K2 tog, repeat to end): 32 stitches.
Change to green.
Row 14: K1 row.
Row 15: P1 row.
Row 16: (K1, K2 tog, repeat to end).
Row 17: Purl row.
Row 18: (K2 tog, repeat to end).
Row 19: Purl.
Row 20: (K2 tog, repeat to end): 10 stitches.

Strawberry hat stalk

Slip remaining stitches onto 3.5 mm (US 10) double-pointed needle, hold with stocking stitch facing you and pull the yarn across the back of the stitches and knit a row.

Turn the knitting so that stocking stitch faces you again and pull the yarn tight across the back, knit another row. Continue to work like this until you have worked 10 rows. Cast off.

Strawberry hat leaves

Cast on 25 stitches.

Row 1: K1, P1, K1, P1, K1, turn, continue on these 5 stitches.

Row 2: K2, P1, K2, turn.

Rows 3–6: Repeat rows 1–2.

Row 7: K2 tog, K 1, K2 tog.

Row 8: K1, P1, K1.

Row 9: K3 tog, slip thread through top loop and secure.

Continue in the same way on each section of 5 stitches until you have 5 leaves.

Stitch up the side of the hat, on the leaves stitch all loose threads into the work and stitch in place around the base of the strawberry stalk. With an aran weight cream wool and starting at the top, make little stitches all around the hat on the outside at even intervals, leaving the yarn to float on the inside. Cast off. Pop onto your jars of jam.

Macaroons

These look so pretty it seems a shame to eat them. Yet the first batch I made I couldn't keep my hands, or rather taste buds, away.

You will need

3 egg whites

25 g (1 oz) caster sugar

½ tsp cream of tartar

Food colouring

125 g (4 oz) ground almonds

225 g (8 oz) icing sugar (confectioners' sugar)

For the chocolate filling

200 g (7 oz) dark chocolate (semisweet), chopped

200 ml (7 fl oz) double cream

1 tsp brandy

15 g (½ oz) unsalted butter

1 Whisk up the egg whites until stiff. Add the caster sugar and the cream of tartar to the egg whites slowly, once incorporated keep whisking until it is smooth and shiny in appearance. Now carefully fold in the food colouring, ground almonds and icing sugar.

2 Line two oven trays with baking parchment and grease lightly. Now using a teaspoon or piping bag place a small amount of the mixture with plenty of space around each one onto the greased sheets, tap the base of the tray to release any air bubbles. Leave them for an hour before baking so a slight skin can form on their surface. Place in the oven at 160°C/320°F/gas mark 2–3 for about 10 to 15 minutes. They are done when the greased paper peels easily from the bottom of each one. Leave to cool.

3 Gently heat the cream and chocolate until the chocolate has just melted, remove form the heat. Add the butter and brandy. Leave to cool for 15 minutes and generously spread onto one side of the macaroons and sandwich with another one. Leave in a fridge to cool for at least half an hour.

Florentines

Don't be put off by the list of ingredients these really are the easiest melt in the mouth treats to make. Although do keep an eye on them when in the oven, they crisp rather quickly and they are rather floppy when first out of the oven so leave them to cool on the baking sheets to cool slightly before carefully lifting with a pallet knife. Cover in chocolate straight away.

You will need

75 g (3 oz) golden syrup

75 g (3 oz) unsalted butter

30 g (1 oz) caster sugar

25 g (1 oz) plain flour (all-purpose flour)

30 g (1 oz) each of: glacé cherries, sultanas, mixed
*   peel, flaked almonds, chopped pistachios*

30 g (1 oz) dark chocolate (semisweet)

30 g (1 oz) milk chocolate

30 g (1 oz) white chocolate

1 Place the butter, caster sugar and syrup into a pan and heat until the butter and sugar have dissolved. Sieve in the flour and add the glace cherries, sultans, mixed peel, flaked almonds, chopped pistachios and pinch of salt. Mix into a paste. Leave to cool for a moment.

2 With a teaspoon place tiny amounts with lots of space around each one onto greased parchment baking trays. Place into 160°C/320°F/gas mark 2–3 oven and cook for 8–10 minutes. Cool on the tray for five minutes and then lift with a pallet knife onto cooling racks. Melt the chocolate over a pan of hot water and leave to cool for a few minutes before spreading on the back of each biscuit. Leave to set in a cool place.

Wrapping

Present these in a ready-made box or construct one yourself, they need to be treated gently and with a little support. The ones I found are meant to be used for baking little loaf cakes, but work perfectly well as a presentation box. Wrap with cellophane and tie with a ribbon.

Not so sweet

Although we tend to think of edible gifts as sweet treats, there are plenty of people out there who don't have a sweet tooth and it would be a shame for them to miss out. I'm sure when you start thinking about it, you'll realise you have plenty of loved ones who would love one of these savoury gifts.

Homemade pasta

The first time I had homemade pasta I was amazed at the ease with which it was made and rolled. The cooking time for pasta this fresh is just a couple of minutes and the texture is silk in your mouth. If you have never tasted homemade pasta make the first batch for yourself.

You will need

350 g (12 oz) strong tipo 00 flour

4 eggs

1 Place the flour either straight onto your tabletop or into a large mixing bowl. Make a well in the centre and add the eggs. Using a fork, beat the eggs until smooth. Gradually start to incorporate some of the flour with the eggs, a little at a time, using your fingertips. Once all the flour has been incorporated, knead the mixture for a few minutes to release all the glutens into the flour. Wrap in cling film and place in the fridge for an hour.

2 When rolling pasta always use lots of pasta flour or semolina as this stops it getting sticky. Remove the pasta dough from the fridge and divide into eight small balls. Sprinkle semolina flour or the pasta flour onto your table and roll the pasta out, then fold in half and roll out again. Repeat about six times. Now roll out as thinly as possible.

3 Cut into strips, squares or any other shapes that you fancy. Leave to dry for about 24 hours, or until the pasta snaps. It can then be stored in an airtight jar or sealed plastic bag. It will last in your store cupboard for about three months.

4 *Alternative method:* If you are using a pasta-rolling machine, roll through the largest setting then fold in half about six times and then slowly take the pasta through the thinner settings, ending with the thinnest.

Wrapping

Make sure that the pasta is thoroughly dried before you package it, then there is no need for it to be refrigerated. It is nice if pasta is wrapped in a clear film so that you can see the produce with a handwritten label attached.

Pesto

Pesto hardly needs an introduction – it has become such a staple. However, nothing quite beats homemade pesto and it's so easy to make, there's no excuse for buying shop-bought ever again!

You will need

100 g (3½ oz) pine nuts
150 g (5½ oz) fresh basil leaves
40 g (1½ oz) Parmesan, grated
1 clove garlic
150 ml (5½ fl oz) extra virgin olive oil
Pinch of salt

1 Toast the pine nuts in a dry pan until slightly coloured. Lightly crush the garlic and salt in a pestle and mortar. Add the toasted pine nuts and grind everything together. Add the basil leaves a few at a time and, working as quickly as possible, pound them into the mixture until you have a paste.

2 Work in the cheese, and then gradually incorporate the oil until it reaches a consistency you like. Reserve a little oil for the top. Spoon the pesto into a jar, and cover the top with the reserved oil. Refrigerate until use.

Wrapping

This has to be given in a glass jar with a tightly sealed lid. Make sure you list all the ingredients on a stick-on label or tie-on tag.

Sun-dried tomato pesto

This variation uses almonds instead of pine nuts and dried tomatoes instead of basil but the essence of the recipe is the same.

You will need

100 g (3½ oz) sun-dried tomatoes

200 g (7 oz) flaked almonds

2 cloves garlic

100 g (3½ oz) Parmesan, grated

200 ml (7 fl oz) olive oil

1 lemon, zest only

Pinch of salt

1 Pour boiling water over the sun-dried tomatoes, leave for 20 minutes, then lightly rinse and pat dry with a paper towel. Toast the almonds in a dry pan. Lightly crush the garlic and salt in a pestle and mortar. Add the roasted almonds to the pestle and mortar and grind everything together.

2 Roughly chop the sun-dried tomatoes and add a few at a time, pounding them into the mixture until you have a paste. Work the cheese and lemon zest in the same way then gradually incorporate the oil until the mixture reaches the desired consistency, reserving a little oil for the top. Spoon the red pesto into a jar and cover the top with oil. Refrigerate until use.

Wrapping

This can only really be given in a glass jar. Make sure you list all the ingredients inside on a label or tag.

Breadsticks

With breadsticks almost anything goes so long as you can get it to stick on the dough before baking. Flavoured oil is a lovely accompaniment to the breadsticks.

You will need

250 g (9 oz) strong flour

1 sachet dried yeast

3 tbsp honey

1 tbsp salt

160 ml (¼ pint) warm water

Selection of sesame seeds, poppy seeds, salt and
*   dried herbs for topping*

1 Preheat the oven to 200°C/400°F/gas mark 6 and grease two baking sheets. Place the flour, yeast, honey and salt in a mixing bowl then mix in the warm water until the mixture forms a dough. Knead for 10 minutes and then cover and leave to rest in a warm place for 1 hour. Knead again and divide into 24 small balls.

2 Roll each small ball into thin cigar-like shapes to the length of your baking tray. Place onto the greased baking trays and leave to rest again for half an hour. Using a pastry brush wet the tops of the sticks with water, twist and curve and sprinkle on the topping of your choice. Bake for 15 minutes or until just golden brown, watch carefully to make sure the sticks don't burn. Cool on a wire tray.

Wrapping

While on holiday in Spain I noticed that the bakeries have rows of hooks with simple drawstring bags full of bread, waiting to be collected. Why not make a simple bag to present your breadsticks in? Simply cut a piece of fabric, fold in half and stitch up the sides. Double fold the top edge over and stitch a hem deep enough to thread a ribbon or length of string through – about 2 cm (¾ in) deep. Thread with ribbon. Tie all the bread sticks into a bundle with a length of raffia and then wrap in some cellophane.

Tasty oils

For flavoured oil use fresh herbs that you have dried yourself. To dry your own herbs, gently rinse them then pat dry, then tie them into small bundles and hang upside down in a dry place. Leave them like this for a few weeks or until the stems break when bent.

You will need

1 litre (2 pints) olive oil
Selection of dried herbs, or one herb you really like
Selection of bottles that can be tightly sealed

1 Sterilize all the bottles by placing in them in boiling hot water for 10 minutes. Dry and then place in a warm oven for 5 minutes to dry completely. The bottles must be completely dry when you pour in the oil.

2 Warm the oil gently in a saucepan. Fill the bottles half way with your chosen herbs and then, using a funnel, top up the bottles with the warmed olive oil. Seal the bottles and place in a dark place for a month before use. This method of infusing oil means it will last for up to a year in the store cupboard.

Wrapping

Present the oils in a range of little glass bottles.

Water biscuits

You will need

85 g (3 oz) plain flour (all-purpose flour)

¼ tsp salt

1 tsp baking powder

45 g (1½ oz) butter

60 ml (2 fl oz) cold water

1 Preheat oven to 180°C/350°F/gas mark 4. Grease and line two baking sheets. Sift the flour, salt and baking powder into a bowl. Rub in the butter until the mixture looks like breadcrumbs. Add the water and mix to form a soft dough. Knead lightly and roll out as thinly as you can on a floured surface.

2 Cut out into the desired shapes and place on baking sheet. Rework the remaining dough until it is all used up.

3 Bake the biscuits in the oven for 15–20 minutes until lightly brown. Place on a wire rack to cool.

Blue cheese and port pâté

The first time I made this was for a friend's birthday and all I had was a portion of Stilton and some port. Thankfully, this simple concoction received nothing but praise.

You will need

500 g (1 lb 2 oz) blue cheese

100 g (3½ oz) unsalted butter, softened

100 ml (3½ fl oz) port wine

150 g (5½ oz) chopped pecan nuts

1 Place the cheese, butter and port in a food processor and pulse a couple of times. Roughly chop the pecan nuts, place in the food processor and pulse for a few seconds.

2 Place the mixture into a bowl and chill in the fridge for a couple of hours.

Living salad bowl

For those friends who love a fresh clean salad this is such a simple gift. It's also ideal for you if you like to garden and spend time nurturing plants. The only real job is choosing which seeds to plant. I think some of the best seed packets on the market are the mixed Italian salad leaves. They are good value as you can grow a variety in one go – the more you pick them the more they grow.

You will need

1 packet of seeds
A small bag of soil
A small garden tray
A warm sunny spot
Water

1 Choose your seeds and follow the instructions on the packet. Water and continue to water every time the soil seems dry.

Wrapping

There are two ways you can present this to friends.

You can make a hand-rolled seed pot with newspaper and garden twine. Once the seeds have germinated in the tray, take a handful of the small seedlings and roll up in the newspaper, twist the end up and tie with a length of garden twine. For friends with a garden this is a perfect gift as the rolls can be planted straight into the garden. Give picking and dressing instructions on the gift tag.

or

Choose a salad bowl for your friend and line it with a layer of thin plastic cut from a bin bag. Once the seeds have germinated and are nearly ready to eat use a knife to cut out a chunk of earth the size of the salad bowl and lay the earth, being careful not to disturb the salad leaves, into the bowl. If the bowl is deep you might need to place some earth into the bottom of the bowl before placing the plants in.

Pickles

The perfect accompaniment to any meal, pickles are easy to make, especially if you have a glut of vegetable produce around at the end of the summer. To sterilize your jars wash them thoroughly and leave in a very low oven for about 20 minutes before adding any hot ingredients. When pouring the hot liquid ingredients into the bottle, place a metal spoon into the jar to conduct the heat. Make sure that all the vegetables are completely covered with the liquid, and cover with a waxed disc while the mixture is still hot. Seal the jars and keep in a cool dark place or in the refrigerator. Jars of homemade pickle always look good with a label giving the ingredients and date that it was made, then topped off with a circles of checked, floral or spotted cloth.

Pickled cucumber

You will need

1 cucumber

1 onion, finely sliced

250 ml (9 fl oz) cider vinegar

1 tsp salt

1 tsp peppercorns

1 tsp coriander seeds

1 tsp turmeric

1 tsp chilli flakes

1 tsp sugar

1 tsp honey

1 Cut the cucumber into slices, sprinkle with salt and leave overnight. Drain off the liquid from the cucumbers. Heat the vinegar, sugar, salt and honey until just boiling and remove from the heat. Layer the cucumber and onion in with the spices and liquid in a warm, sterile jar.

Pickled beetroot

You will need

8–10 small beetroots

200 ml (7 fl oz) rice wine vinegar

1 tsp sugar

2 bay leaves

12 peppercorns

1 Boil the beetroots for about an hour until soft and peel. Heat the vinegar and sugar until just boiling then remove from heat.

2 Place the beetroots in the warm, sterile jar, add in the bay leaves and peppercorns. Pour in the warm vinegar mixture.

Pickled red cabbage

You will need

½ red cabbage

200 ml (7 fl oz) rice vinegar/sherry

1 red onion, finely sliced

1 tsp allspice

2 tsp light brown caster sugar

1 Shred the cabbage into very thin slices and layer in a bowl with salt. Leave overnight. The cabbage will produce liquid, which must be drained off. Rinse the cabbage. Heat the vinegar, sugar and allspice until just boiling and remove from the heat. Layer the cabbage with the sliced red onion and the spices from the mix in a warm, sterile jar.

Pickled egg

You will need

6 eggs

200 ml (7 fl oz) rice vinegar

1 tbsp sugar

1 tsp salt

8 cloves

1 Boil the eggs for about seven minutes until hard-boiled. Peel and place in cool water. Heat up the vinegar, sugar and salt until both have dissolved in the vinegar. Remove from the heat. Place the eggs in a warm, sterile jar, add cloves and allspice and pour in the vinegar.

Marinated olives

This has to be one of easiest gifts to make. Although olives are great just as they are, for a special treat marinate for a few hours – the longer they are left the more the flavours will develop. These will all keep in the fridge for up to a week. Do make sure you give instructions on bringing to room temperature before consuming.

Black chilli and orange

You will need

Olives

Rind of 1 orange

1 tsp dried chilli

Olive oil to cover

1 Tip the olives into a bowl and add the zest of the orange and the chilli. Cover in light olive oil and toss to combine the flavours and leave to marinate in a cool place for a week.

Green olives

You will need

4 sun-dried tomatoes, finely sliced

4 cloves garlic, finely sliced

Olive oil to cover

1 Finely slice the garlic and dried tomatoes and add to the olives. Cover in light olive oil and toss together to combine the flavours and leave to marinate in a cool place for a week.

Mixed large olives

You will need

½ tsp fennel and cumin seeds

1 tsp coriander seeds

1 lemon

Sprig of rosemary

Sprig of thyme

3 bay leaves

Olive oil to cover

1 Finely peel the lemon and place the peel in a bowl. Add the olives. Dry-fry the coriander, fennel and cumin seeds in a hot skillet or frying pan for a couple of minutes. Add to the olives and lemon peel while still hot. Wash and dry the fresh herbs and add to the bowl. Cover in light olive oil and toss together to combine the flavours and leave to marinate in a cool place for a week.

Wrapping

Find the most interesting glass jars with a lid that seals well. To be really indulgent why not give your friends a good bottle of wine to accompany the treat. Olives somehow always marry well with wine; it must be the heat in which these tiny little fruit grow.

Tasty salts

Salt. What a fantastic substance – without it all our food would taste bland. This is another recipe that can be adjusted according to taste. I have given you the ingredients and weights below for nine different salts, yet this really is about personal taste. These salts can be used for a variety of dishes or just rubbed into meat or fish before cooking or to marinate. You can either mix these before pouring into the jar or layer for a more unusual look. Any seeds have been dry roasted first to release their unique flavours. Try to source a good-quality sea salt crystal for the base as it tastes better.

Gamaso salt – for sprinkling onto rice dishes

6 tsp sesame seeds
6 tsp salt

Garlic salt – for adding to the pot

8 tsp salt
4 tsp dried garlic

Curry salt – touch of spice

1 tsp coriander (lightly crushed)
1 tsp cumin (lightly crushed)
6 tsp salt
1 tsp garam masala

Chilli salt – for meat with heat

4 tsp dried chilli flakes
8 tsp salt
Layer the salt with the chilli flakes.

Sweet smoked paprika salt – for classic patatas bravas

4 tsp smoked sweet paprika
8 tsp salt

Salt and pepper – for the table

4 tsp freshly ground pepper
8 tsp salt
Layer the pepper in first, then add the salt.

Lemongrass and kaffir leaf salt – taste of South East Asia

3 tsp chopped kaffir lime leaf

3 tsp chopped lemongrass

6 tsp salt

Chinese five spice salt – perfect for belly of pork

3 tsp Chinese five spice powder

8 tsp of salt

Wrapping

Place the salts in tiny glass jars to see all the colours of the contents, make paper twists in greaseproof paper or fill a salt pig with a mixture of flavours.

Two sauces in a pack

These sauces are great accompaniments to roast meat – traditionally cranberry sauce is for turkey and mint sauce for lamb. I have kept the recipes simple, although I have added a hint of chilli to the mint sauce. If chilli is not your thing, it works just as well without.

Cranberry sauce

You will need

250 g (9 oz) cranberries

60 g (2½ oz) caster sugar

2 clementines

Peel of 1 clementine

1 Place the climentines and peel into a food processor and process until pulp. Place a sieve onto a medium sized saucepan and strain the juice out of the fruit. Add the sugar and dissolve in the juice over medium heat. Stir in the cranberries and cook until the cranberries start to pop (about 10 minutes).

2 Remove from heat, leave to cool for 20 minutes and then pour into sterilized jars.

Mint sauce

You will need

1 kg (2 lb 2 oz) apples

750 ml (1⅓ pint) water

150 ml (¼ pint) vinegar

60 g (2½ oz) fresh mint, chopped

175 g (6 oz) caster sugar

2 tsp dried chilli flakes.

1 Peel and core the apples and place into a large saucepan. Add a little of the measured water and cook for 20 minutes until soft and easy to mash, then add the chilli. Place the apple pulp into a sieve and let the juice drain into a bowl – this will take a couple of hours. Finely chop the mint and add to the rest of the water and sugar, and bring to the boil in a saucepan. Take off the heat and leave to cool.

2 Add the strained apple juice and vinegar and then bring to the boil. Add the vinegar and simmer for about 40 minutes stirring occasionally. Leave to cool for 20 minutes then pour into sterilized jars.

Wrapping

Once in their jars, either present as they are or take a look around to see if you can find a box the pair will sit in comfortably. You could also use a photograph of the raw ingredients to make labels so you don't have to explain what's inside the jar.

Plum and apple chutney

I have a lovely plum tree in my back garden, yet every year after eating as many plums as we can, we are still left with a glut so I always make chutney. This year I was given a pile of apples from my neighbour's garden so you could say this is a gift made from a gift.

You will need

1 kg (2 lb 2 oz) plums
1 kg (2 lb 2 oz) apples
500 g (1 lb) red onions
500 g (1 lb) soft brown sugar
500 ml (1 pint) cider vinegar
250 g (9 oz) dried fruit, such as dates, apricots or
    prunes (use just one or a mixture)
75 g (3 oz) freshly grated ginger
3 tsp cumin seeds, dry-roasted and ground
3 tsp black peppercorns, roughly ground
1 tsp salt
1 tsp dried chilli flakes

1 Stone the plums, peel and core the apples and peel the onions. Roughly chop everything together. Chop the dried fruit into small pieces.

2 Place all the ingredients into a large saucepan and bring to a gentle simmer. Cover and simmer for 2 to 2½ hours, or until the mixture is thick, dark brown in colour and reduced in quantity. When you scrape a wooden spoon across the bottom of the pan the chutney should stay apart.

3 Leave to rest and cool slightly before decanting into clean, sterile jam jars.

Wrapping

This is a gift that needs to be presented in a glass jar, although I like the idea of adding a beautiful portion of cheese to give with the pickle. Why not tie the cheese to the top of the lid and then wrap the whole lot in cellophane?

Drinks

A bottle of homemade cordial or limoncello
or a beautifully presented mulled wine bag makes a perfect gift
for anyone who likes the finer things in life.

Elderflower cordial

You can add vodka to the cordial to make a delicious grown-up liqueur.

You will need

20 elderflower heads

1.5 litres (2½ pints) filtered water

1.5 kg (3 lb 5 oz) sugar

1 unwaxed lemon, sliced

20 g (1 oz) citric acid

500 ml (1 pint) vodka (optional)

1 It is said that's its best to pick elderflowers when the blooms are in full sun and to make sure you are near to where you are going to make the cordial as the flowers need to be used within 1–2 hours of picking. You need to pick about 20 flower heads and shake off all the insects. Place the flower heads into a large bucket.

2 Boil the water in a pan and add the sugar, then stir until the sugar has dissolved. Pour the sugar solution over the flower heads then add the lemon and citric acid and stir. Leave to steep overnight or for 24 hours.

3 Use a fine sieve or muslin cloth to get the last of the insects out. Decant into clean sterilized bottles and keep in a cool place. As a non-alcoholic drink for children, it will need to be diluted with water and instructions given accordingly. For your adult friends, dilute 500 ml (18 fl oz) of your elderflower cordial with 500 ml (18 fl oz) of vodka (this amount can be adapted according to taste). Mix well, bottle and keep in the fridge until ready to give away.

Wrapping

There are loads of interesting glass vessels on the market that you could use – just make sure that the bottle is watertight. On the internet you can buy all sorts of cork sizes, which means that glass vases can also be utilized for bottling your produce as presents. These have the added advantage that your gift will have another life as a vase when the contents have been drunk.

Tea infusions

This kind of tea really needs to be served in a bone china cup with a saucer. When made, the brew needs to be clear and pure in colour. The bottom of the cup needs to be just visible through the hot liquid. There are no rules on the added flavors although you do need to use ingredients that will dry and yet still retain their original taste.

You will need

1 unwaxed lemon

1 unwaxed orange

1 unwaxed lime

Packet of loose leaf tea

Here are a few flavours that you could experiment with:

For stronger flavoured teas

Orange

Lemon

Lime

Lemongrass

For medium flavoured teas

Chinese allspice

Star anise

Cinnaman

Cranberries

Fresh ginger

For milder flavoured teas

Mint

Thyme

Rosemary

Chamomile

1 Thinly slice the lemon, orange and lime and leave to dry, either on a radiator or in a very low oven. The orange might need to be cut into quarters. The important thing is that the fruit is totally dried out before being mixed with the tea.

2 For each tea serving you will need 1 heaped teaspoon of loose leaf tea, a few slices of lemon,

orange or lime and a sprinkling or pinch of your chosen flavouring.

Wrapping

You will need half a metre of voile or other fine cloth. Cut the cloth into squares 20 x 20 cm (8 x 8 in). Mix the flavoured teas you would like to give and place them in the centre of each square. Fold the edges of the square inwards so that the raw edges meet in the centre. Fold the cloth again so that the raw edges are encased inside a long strip of cloth. Now fold the cloth for the final time so that the two raw edges that are left meet at the top. Secure the top edge with a cocktail stick about 1 cm (½ in) from the top using it like a sewing needle. For a really special gift, present the tea bags in their own pretty china cup.

Cocktails

Cocktails are always a treat and an indulgence to drink. For a friend's 40th birthday I presented him with a small cocktail shaker full of a cocktail, ready to have ice added, shaken and poured. Around the neck of the bottle I had bought a set of letters from our local bead shop that spelt out his name, as if this particular cocktail was named after him.

FROSTING THE GLASS

Not all cocktails demand this service although it's always special to drink from a glass that is edged. There are two ways to edge the lip of the glass. Choose either salt or sugar depending on the drink you are making and sprinkle it onto a flat plate. Cut a lemon or lime in half and run the cut edge around the lip of the glass. Place the glas upside down into the plate of either salt or sugar and then leave to set. Placing the glass into the freezer will help with this. You can also dip the rim into orange juice or grenadine, which will turn the sugar red.

Champagne and flower cocktail

Any soft fruit, edible sweet flowers or light spices marinated in vodka syrup for a few weeks will pep up a bottle of fizz and make the most wonderful champagne/cava/prosseco cocktail.

You will need

Handful of edible flowers

200 g (7 oz) caster sugar

Small bottle of champagne or prosecco

1 First make the flower syrup. Select the flowers you wish to use and place them in a 500 ml (1 pint) jar, two-thirds of the way up. Remember to remove the stamen and the stalks of the flowers. Place the sugar in a heavy-based pan and add 120 ml (4 fl oz) water. Heat until the sugar melts and dissolves. Leave to cool for 10 minutes.

2 Place a metal spoon into the jar to help conduct the heat so as not to break the glass and pour the syrup into the jar over the fruit. Leave in a dark place for a couple of weeks to steep.

Wrapping

To make a champagne cocktail, place a few syrup-drenched flowers in a champagne glass and add a sugar lump. Add a tablespoonof brandy and top with the fizz. For a gift I like to put together a small bottle of fizz, a jar of edible flowers in syrup and a measure of brandy. Don't forget to include instructions on how to make the cocktail!

Cocktails in measures

You can choose any cocktail your friends might like, it's just a question of premeasuring out the liquid, pouring the measurements into test tubes or mini shakers and writing a list of how you pour it, how much ice you need to use and whether it needs to be shaken or stirred. If the desired cocktail requires fresh juice you could either give the fruit to your friend or use long life fruit juice.

Bartender

You will need

20 ml (⅔ fl oz) dry vermouth

20 ml (⅔ fl oz) sweet vermouth

20 ml (⅔ fl oz) gin

20 ml (⅔ fl oz) medium dry sherry

5 ml (⅛ fl oz) grand mariner

A twist of orange peel

Mix all the tubes together with ice and then strain into cocktail glass. Use a sugar frosted glass with orange juice fixing the sugar.

Margarita

You will need

30 ml (1 fl oz) tequila

15 ml (½ fl oz) triple sec

10 ml (⅓ fl oz) fresh lime juice

Shake all the tubes with ice, strain and pour. Use a salt frosted glass.

Tequila sunrise

You will need

60 ml (2 fl oz) tequila

10 ml ((⅓ fl oz) grenadine

100 ml (3½ fl oz) orange juice

Pour the tequila over ice, add the orange juice and then pour in the grenadine last so that it sinks to the bottom. Use a sugar frosted glass with grenadine to fix the sugar.

Blue heaven

You will need

30 ml (1 fl oz) white rum

15 ml (½ fl oz) blue curacao

15 ml (½ fl oz) amaretto

15 ml (½ fl oz) fresh lime juice

75 ml (2½ fl oz) pineapple juice

5 ml (⅛ fl oz) sugar syrup

Mix all tubes together with ice and strain into tall glass. Use a sugar frosted glass with blue curaco or cream demonth to fix the sugar.

Limoncello

I was given this recipe in a rather strange way; I was in my local supermarket with a basket full of lemons when the woman in front of me asked if I was making limoncello. I said no, lemonade, but would love to know how to make limoncello, whereupon she promptly gave me her Italian mother-in-law's recipe. I wrote it down on an old receipt and now limoncello has been enjoyed by many a friend since. So thank you to that stranger in the supermarket.

You will need

10 unwaxed lemons

*1 litre (2 pints) vodka or other strong clear alcohol
(at least 40%)*

500 g (1 lb 2 oz) sugar

½ litre (1 pint) filtered water

1 Using a potato peeler remove all the peel from the lemons, making sure you only peel off the yellow peel and not too much of the white pith. Place into a large kilner jar with the litre of alcohol and leave to soak for 10 days. Turn the jar every other day and the liquid will soon become acid yellow in colour.

2 On the tenth day, strain out the lemon peel and add the water and sugar. Leave for another ten days turning the jar every other day. On day ten it will be ready to drink, although I advise you to place it in the fridge for a few hours first, as it is always best served very cold.

Wrapping

You need to source some nice glass bottles. So the receiver knows that the content is lemon based add a label to its neck that explains the ingredients. This really does need to be consumed when it is ice cold.

Sloe gin and sloe gin chocolate

My mother's advice is to give it a sip every so often to make sure it tastes the way you like it. She also believes that it's best to prick the sloes with a silver fork. I love tradition even if it's made up, so this small ceremony is now vital to the end result – a delicious bottle of ruby-red nectar.

You will need

400 g (14 oz) sloes

1 litre (2 pints) gin

200 g (7 oz) caster sugar

400 g (14 oz) dark chocolate (semisweet)

pinch of sea salt crystals

1 Sloes are said to be ripe for picking after the first frost, but be careful as the bushes have sharp thorns. Wash and then prick your sloes and drop them into a large glass bottle. Add 2–3 tablespoons of caster sugar, depending on your taste. Top up the bottle with gin and cork or seal. Place the bottle in a dark cupboard and once a week turn the bottle so that the sloes have a chance to release their juices.

2 The sloes need to be left in the gin for about two months before you strain them. During this process taste the sloe gin, adding more sugar if you wish. When the sloe gin is ready, strain the sloes from the gin through some fine muslin and a sieve, keeping the sloes to one side. Decant the gin into desired gift bottles. These can be any sort of shape or size as long as the lid fits securely.

3 To make the sloe gin chocolate, chop the reserved sloes into small pieces and remove the stones. Melt the chocolate and pour into a small tray lined with baking parchment or into individual chocolate moulds. Sprinkle the gin-drenched fruit onto the melted chocolate and then add a tiny sprinkling of salt crystals. Leave to set.

Wrapping

Decant the sloe gin into a bottle, add a 'Drink-me' label, then wrap the sloe gin slab with clear cellophane. Wrap a wide strip of card or thick paper around the chocolate, stating where the sloes were picked, on what day and when you made the sloe gin.

Christmas gifts

What better time to give edible gifts than Christmas? In this chapter you will find
sweet-toothed treats for all ages, as well as some savoury ideas.
Try Turkish delight with its soft squidgy middle and sugar mice nestled in a cozy cot of
edible rice paper bedding. They are perfect tucked in the toe of a Christmas stocking.
Finally there are rich, booze-infused truffles from a very special recipe.
Christmas just wouldn't be Christmas without chocolate truffles.

Edible gift tags

These dried fruit leathers can be placed in an envelope of parchment paper and are ideal for sending in the post. I hate throwing away the little tags and messages that family and friends send on gifts but now you can let your friend's consume or eat your words!

You will need

2 tbsp hot water

1 tsp gelatine powder

*125 g (4 oz) dried fruit (you can use any dried
    fruit and if you keep them separately you will
    have a colour pallet to work with).*

Mixture of dried fruits for decorating with

Rice paper

A range of tiny biscuit cutters

Marzipan

1 In a small bowl sprinkle the gelatine powder into the hot water, whisk well and leave for 5 minutes for the gelatine to dissolve.

2 Puree the fruit in a food processer until it resembles small crumbs, add the dissolved gelatine and puree to a soft texture.

3 Tip the pureed fruit out onto a sheet of baking parchment and place another sheet of parchment on the top. Using a rolling pin gently rollout to a very thin sheet. It needs to end up approximately 2 mm (⅛ in) in depth when using it for the base of your card. It can be slightly thiner if being used for cutting out shapes with biscuit cutters for decorating. Place onto a wire tray and carefully peel off the top sheet of parchment paper. Leave in a warm place to dry for 10 to 20 hours.

4 Once dry, cut the thinner fruit sheet into the required shape for your gift tag or card and using edible glue stick it onto a sheet of rice paper also cut to size. Now the fun begins. If you have made leathers with different fruit you will have some colours to play with. Use one as your base and cut out the others with the biscuit cutter.

Wrapping

Using parchment paper cut out enough to wrap up your card and either secure with sellotape or edible glue. When sending in the post it is best to slip a sheet of card in behind your edible card to make sure that it won't get bent in transit.

Mulled wine bags

One form or other of this warming mix of wine steeped in aromatic spices is presented to friends all over Europe during the festive season; Germany has Gluhwein, Scandinavia has glogg, Romania has vin fiert and we have mulled wine. All you need to do is collect together your chosen spices and put them into a hand-stitched pouch or bag.

You will need

1 cinnamon stick

3 star anises

Few shavings of nutmeg

½ vanilla pod

1 slice of dried orange

8 sugar cubes

6 cloves

Muslin or fine cotton fabric

Embroidery thread

1 The bag will need to be large enough to hold the largest ingredients. Make the bag by cutting out a circle of fabric about 20 cm (8 in) in diameter. Use a needle and some embroidery thread to do a running stitch 1 cm (½ in) in from the edge, all the way round.

2 Place the ingredients in the centre of the circle and then gently pull the thread to draw the material up into a bag. Secure the thread well, leaving a length of thread long enough to tie around the neck of a bottle.

Wrapping

Tie the bag around the neck of a bottle of wine or cider. Simply tell the recipient to pour the wine into a large pan, add the muslin bag and heat gently for about 30 minutes.

Turkish delight

Coated in a dusting of snowy icing sugar, hidden in layers of tissue paper in a bejewelled box… there is nothing quite like the soft texture and the essence of rose in your mouth when you taste Turkish delight.

You will need

225 g (8 oz) caster sugar

1½ tbsp lime juice

40 ml (1½ fl oz) water

1 tbsp powdered gelatin dissolved in 40 ml (1½ fl oz) warm water

30 g (1 oz) cornflour (corn starch)

½ tsp rosewater

Few drops red food colouring

40 g (1½ oz) icing sugar (confectioners' sugar)

1 Line a square cake tin with liberally oiled greaseproof paper.

2 Place the lime juice, water and sugar in a heavy-based saucepan then heat gently until the sugar has melted; bring to a gentle boil for a few minutes. Remove from the heat and leave to cool for a few minutes, then add the gelatin and cornflour. Stir well until it comes back to the boil. Let it boil for about 30 seconds. Remove from the heat and thoroughly stir in the rosewater and food colouring.

3 Pour the mixture into your prepared cake tin and leave to set for a few hours. Turn out onto a surface lightly dusted with icing sugar and cut into squares or chunks. Dust liberally with sifted icing sugar.

Wrapping

Paint an empty box however you like. When dry, coat with acrylic varnish. Now enjoy yourself by glueing jewels and shiny beads all over the box.

Sugar mice

These little mice look so cute, it seems a shame to wake them up or eat them. They are the easiest things to make, literally water and sugar, yet the fondant does have a point of no return. It's a weird sort of sugar science, but not complicated. You just have to use a jam-making thermometer and be really careful of the hot sugar. You will need mice-shaped moulds for this recipe.

You will need

400 g (14 oz) granulated sugar

200 ml (7 fl oz) water

30 ml (1 fl oz) liquid glucose

Few drops food colouring

String for tails

1 Place the sugar, water and liquid glucose into a heavy-based saucepan and bring to the boil. The temperature needs to reach 115°C/240°F. You must use a sugar thermometer to test the temperature. When the sugar reaches the right temperature, remove the pan from the heat and leave to stand for about five minutes to cool slightly.

2 Add the food colouring and stir very gently until the mixtxure turns slightly milky. While still liquid, pour into mice moulds, being very careful not to splash yourself. Lay the tails in place. They will set very quickly so you can see the beauty of your work within 20 minutes. Depending on the mould size you should have about six mice.

Wrapping

Take a few sheets of rice paper and shred into strips to make a layer of bedding. I put mine through the paper shredder and it worked very well. Place the edible shredded paper in a plain cardboard box tied with string.

Chocolate truffles

These is my dad's truffles recipe. I found the recipe written on a slip of paper in one of his cookbooks after he died and I've been making them at Christmas ever since. Every year they all get eaten and everyone loves them.

You will need

200 g (7 oz) dark chocolate (semisweet)
75 g (2½ oz) unsalted butter
75 ml (2½ oz) double cream
1 egg yolk
1 tbsp brandy
Pinch of salt

1 Break the chocolate into squares. Heat it in a bowl set over simmering water. When the chocolate has melted, take it from the heat and add the butter and cream. When the butter and cream have melted, add the egg yolk and brandy.

2 Lightly beat to thicken and add a pinch of salt. Leave the truffle mixture to cool and then place in the fridge for at least an hour to harden. This makes it easier to handle and form into round bite-sized pieces.

3 Spoon up a full teaspoon and roll into small balls with the tips of your fingers – don't use your palms as they are much hotter than your fingers. Once this is done you can roll the portions in cocoa powder or nuts (see cover picture) seeds or desiccated coconut – just use your imagination.

4 If you want to roll them in chocolate, place them back in the fridge to cool.

5 Melt your chosen chocolate coating in a double boiler or in a bowl over a pan of boiling water. Once melted, leave to rest away from the heated water for a few minutes.

6 Temper the chocolate with a pastry scraper before rolling the truffles. Pour the melted chocolate onto a flat surface and move it around with a pastry scraper to help cool it down.

7 You could also roll the truffles in different coloured edible gold leaf.

Wrapping

You will need

Small boxes

Scissors

Tissue paper

Ribbon

Trimmings

Petit four cases

A beautiful box of chocolates, tied with a bow, always makes a welcome gift. There are many empty boxes on the market that can be bought and decorated. Keep it simple by painting the box in one colour and when dry decorate with cutouts from pictures, wrapping paper and magazines. Alternatively, look out for small boxes for individual chocolates, or try making one yourself. Put a layer of tissue paper in the bottom of the box and place the truffles in the paper cases nestled inside. Add the lid and then decorate with ribbons and bows.

Roasted nuts

You can use anything that you fancy to flavour your nuts, let your imagination run wild, but do remember to keep the oil, sugar or sugar syrup weights in place. Try freshly grated Parmesan cheese, sea salt and freshly cracked pepper, dried herb mix or a sweet version. The nuts can be stored in an airtight container for up to 10 days. Here are four variations.

200 g (7 oz) pecan nuts

3 tsp sweet smoked paprika

3 tsp salt crystals

2 tbsp olive oil

Few grinds of mixed pepper corns

1 tbsp caster sugar

200 g (7 oz) almonds

1 tbsp cayenne pepper

3 tsp salt

3 tsp fennel seeds slightly crushed in a pestle and mortar

1 tbsp maple syrup

2 tbsp olive oil

200 g (7 oz) sunflower seeds

1 tbsp soy sauce

3 tsp wasabi powder

¼ sheet of toasted nori shredded into fine pieces

1 tbsp peanut oil

1 tsp sesame oil

3 teaspoon of grated palm sugar

200 g (7 oz) hazelnuts

2 tsp salt

2 tsp roughly ground coriander seeds

2 tsp garam masala

1 tsp chilli flakes

2 tbsp peanut oil

1 tsp dried garlic powder

1 Rinse the nuts first.

2 Place nuts in a baking tray. Roast at 180°C/350°F/gas mark 4 for 10–15 minutes and then remove from the oven. Place the other ingredients into a small saucepan and heat until the sugar has just melted.

3 Now pour the hot mixture over the nuts, mixing really well making sure all the nuts are totally coated.

4 Leave to cool.

Wrapping

These cellophane cone wraps are really easy to make. Cut a circle of the cellophane using a large dinner plate or saucepan lid. You could also use scissors with a wavy or zigzag edge. Cut the circles in half and roll into a cone. Fill the cones up and and sticky tape into place. Fold the very end point over by 2 cm (¾ in) to stop the nuts falling out and secure in place. Of course you could always buy bags.

Christmas tree biscuits

These delightful biscuits make lovely Christmas gifts. Not only do they look beautiful hanging from a Christmas tree, they also taste good too. They should keep hanging on a tree for a week.

You will need

120 g (4 oz) butter or margarine

60 g (2 oz) caster sugar

2 eggs

300 g (10 oz) plain flour (all-purpose flour)

Pinch salt

2 tsp orange essence

1 Cream together the butter and sugar until pale in colour. Beat in the egg and then fold in the flour and salt and essence. Mix together until you have a soft pliable dough. Wrap in clingfilm and refrigerate for at least 15 minutes.

2 Preheat the oven to 180°C/350°F/gas mark 4. On a floured surface, roll out the dough to a thickness of 3 mm (¼ in) and cut out your desired shapes. Place your biscuits onto a baking tray lined with baking paper. Using a smaller cutter or a skewer, make a hole at the top of you biscuits so that when baked and cool you can thread ribbon through to hang them up.

3 Cook in the oven for about 15 minutes, or until lightly golden in colour. Remove from the oven and use a pallet knife to transfer to a cooling rack.

Decorating and giftwrapping

You will need

1 egg white

250 g (9 oz) icing sugar (confectioners' sugar)

Edible glitter and other edible decorations

Piping bag with fine nozzle

Short lengths of ribbon to thread through the
*   biscuits*

Cellophane for wrapping

1 Using the egg white like glue, sprinkle the glitter and other edible goodies onto the biscuits.

Leave them to one side for a couple of hours.

2 Sieve the icing sugar into a bowl and add a few tablespoons of water at a time, mixing until you have a reasonably stiff white icing. Place the icing into a piping bag and then pipe around your biscuits. Try any designs and patterns that you like – there are no rules to this. It can be a little messy to begin with – particularly if children are helping you. Either place in individual cellophane bags or present a tin and help your friends to deck out their tree.

Gingerbread men

These biscuits have quite a history. The first gingerbread dough biscuits were seen in medieval times. By the sixteenth century, gingerbread dough was being moulded into figures. It is said that Queen Elizabeth 1 of England gave gingerbread figurines in the likeness of her most important guests at her large banquets. Gingerbread men also shot to fame in the 1800s because of the children's folk story. He generally has a smile and buttons down his front.

You will need

60 g (2 oz) caster sugar

60 g (2 oz) soft dark brown sugar

100 g (3½ oz) butter

1 egg

3 tsp ground ginger

1 tsp ground cinnamon

140 g (4½ oz) honey

2 tsp bicarbonate of soda (baking soda)

Pinch of salt

240 g (9 oz) plain flour (all-purpose flour)

1 egg white

500 g (1 lb) icing sugar (confectioners' sugar)

1 Place sugars and butter in a bowl and cream together. Softly beat in the egg and spices and honey then mix in the flour to form a soft dough. Turn out onto a floured surface and knead gently until smooth. Wrap in clingfilm and refrigerate for about 15 minutes.

2 Preheat the oven to 180°C/350°F/gas mark 4. Unwrap the dough and roll out on a floured surface to a thickness of about 3 mm (¼ in). Using a gingerbread man cutter, make as many little men as you can and place on a baking tray lined with baking parchment. Reform and roll the uncut dough and cut more shapes, repeating until all the dough is used up.

3 Cook in the preheated oven for 15–20 minutes until golden in colour. Cool for a few minutes and then when slightly hardened move to a cooling rack.

4 Make royal icing by sieving the icing sugar into a bowl. Lightly whisk the egg white and stir into the icing sugar until you have a stiff icing. Decorate your gingerbread men with the icing.

Wrapping

Once the icing has set, tie a little bow around the neck of each one so that they look ready for any occasion. There is nothing like a whole tin of biscuits so search the shops for just the right size tin and place your little men inside. The gift is also a tin for future treats. Or you could build a gingerbread house and place your gingerbread men stacked up inside.

Gingerbread house

This is such fun to make, although you do need a little experience with using a piping bag and even a second pair of hands to hold it together while the icing sets. How you share and divide this cake I have no idea, but it does make a lovely centrepiece for the table.

You will need

700 g (1½ lb) self raising flour

2 tsp mixed spice

2 tsp ground ginger

2 tbsp lemon juice

Zest of a lemon

350 g (11 oz) soft brown sugar

150 g (5 oz) golden syrup

80 g (3 oz) butter

2 eggs, beaten

2 egg whites

500 g (1 lb) icing sugar (confectioners' sugar)

1 tsp lemon juice

1 tsp glycerine

Nuts and dried fruits, to decorate

1 Cut out all the paper templates (page 175).

    2 Sieve the flour and spices into a large bowl and add the lemon zest. Melt the butter in a pan with the syrup and then add to the flour with the beaten egg and lemon juice. Mix until you have a soft dough.

    3 Preheat the oven to 180°C/350°F/gas mark 4. Turn the dough onto a floured surface and bring it together by kneading slightly. Cut into four equal amounts. Grease four sheets of baking parchment. Liberally flour the greased baking parchment and roll out one piece of dough on the paper to a rectangle about 20 x 30 cm (8 x 12 in). Because this is on the paper it will be easier to transport to the baking tray. Place into oven and cook for 20–25 minutes. Keep an eye on it as you don't want the corners to burn. If you have a large enough oven and enough trays you can cook all the pieces at the same time, if not, cook and cut each piece separately.

4 When the gingerbread is cooked, carefully lift the baking parchment from the tray to a flat surface. Be ready with your templates as the parts need to be cut out while the cake biscuit is still warm. Lay your paper template onto the biscuit and cut with a long knife using downward action. Carefully lift to a cooling tray.

5 Once all the pieces are baked, cut and cooled, you are ready to ice and assemble your house. Mix together the egg whites, icing sugar, lemon juice and glycerine until you have a stiff paste. When not using the icing keep covered with cling film to stop it from drying out. Just use the icing like glue. It's easier if you place the icing into an icing bag with a small nozzle, you will have more control. Before gluing my house together I iced on some of the details, while it was flat on the table.

6 Start with the roof and put ice on your tiles. Before the icing sets stick on your roof tile decorations. I used pine nuts at each iced roof tile joint but any edible fruit or nuts will do. Now ice on the windows and decide where the door will be. You are now ready to fix the house together.

7 Start with gluing the gable ends to the sides of the house with the icing. You will need to hold this in place for a few minutes or until it seems it will stay in place. Now pipe the icing on the top edges of the structure ready to set the roof in place. Again hold in place until it seems set.

8 Once the house is fully assembled, you can pipe more icing around the joins for extra strength.

Wrapping

The house needs to be completely covered and wrapped so it's a total surprise for the recipient. A rather hard item to wrap for transportation, I managed to find a large white box which fitted over the cake board and just skimmed the almond roof ridge so the house.

Gingerbread house templates

Illustrations are not drawn to scale.

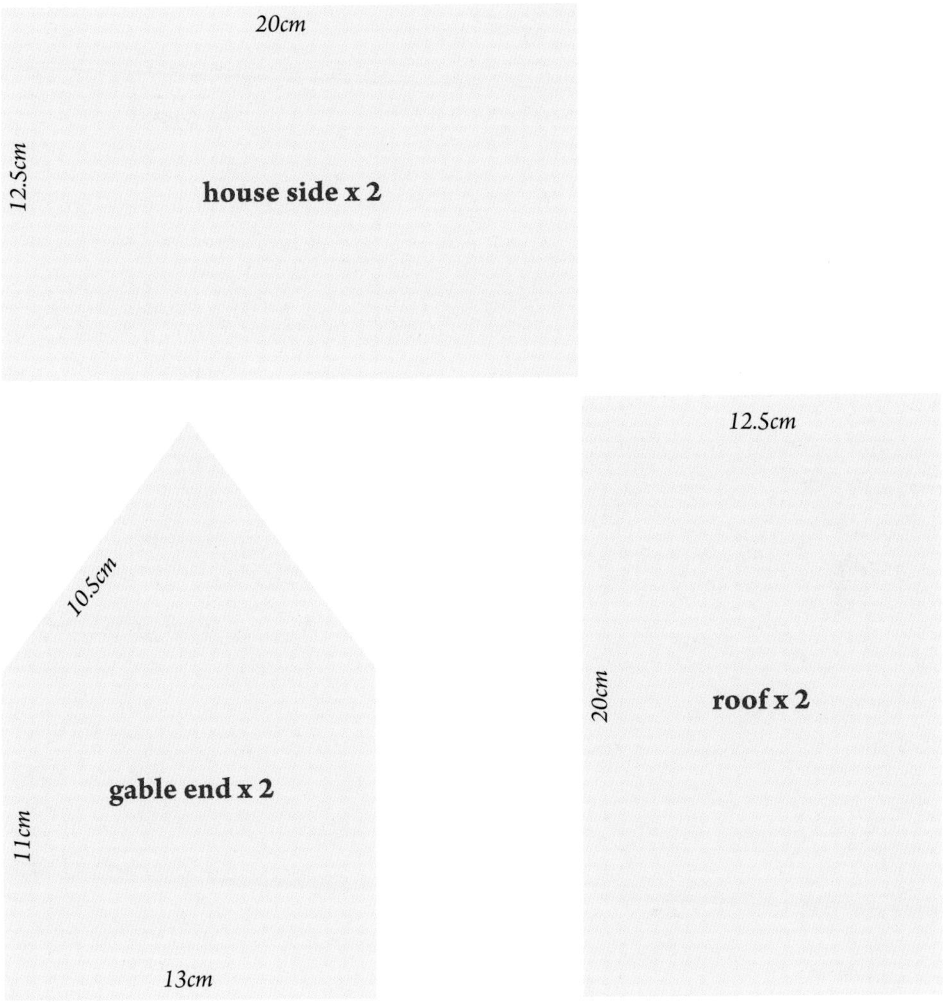

20cm

12.5cm

house side x 2

10.5cm

11cm

gable end x 2

13cm

12.5cm

20cm

roof x 2

To my mum, for not minding if I made a mess.

With thanks to Debbie, Julie and Andrea, you all know what you did. To Derek from First Leaf for his advice on edible flowers, Steve at Gold Leaf Supplies for his delicate edible gold leaf samples and to Steamer Trading for the loan of kitchen props.

About the author

Jane Lyster is a working artist who can turn her hand to any made project. After completing a fine art textile degree, she discovered many different materials and media. At the same time, she became a carnival artist, working on street-based art, encouraging the public to dress up and to make each other laugh. Part of this celebratory work included large embroidered banner backdrops for a speech by Her Majesty Queen Elizabeth. For twenty years she lectured at an art college, delivering a varied programme including drawing, photography, fashion and textiles. She was launch editor of *Making*, a magazine about contemporary crafts in the home, and has since worked as a food technician on several major films such as *W.E*, Madonna's film about King Edward VIII and Wallis Simpson, and *The Iron Lady*, with Meryl Streep. She lives on the south-east coast of England with her husband and two not-so-small sons.

First published in 2012 by New Holland Publishers
London • Sydney • Cape Town • Auckland
www.newhollandpublishers.com
www.newholland.com.au

Garfield House, 86–88 Edgware Road, London W2 2EA United Kingdom
Unit 1, 66 Gibbes Street, Chatswood, NSW 2067, Australia
Wembly Square, First Floor, Solan Street Gardens, Cape Town 8000 South Africa
218 Lake Road, Northcote, Auckland, New Zealand

Text copyright © 2012 Jane Lyster

Photography copyright © 2012 New Holland Publishers
Copyright © 2012 New Holland Publishers

Jane Lyster has asserted her moral right to be identified as the author of this work.

A catalogue record for this book is available from the British Library and the National Library of Australia.

ISBN 978 178009 043 6

Publisher: Clare Sayer
Publishing Manager: Lliane Clarke
Design: Celeste Vlok
Photography: Tim Clinch
Production Manager: Olga Dementiev
Printed by: Toppan Leefung Printing Ltd China

10 9 8 7 6 5 4 3 2 1